# LET'S GET THIS
# PARTY
# STARTED!

DIY Celebrations for You &
Your Kids to Create Together

## SOLEIL MOON FRYE

photographs by meeno

Published in 2013 by Stewart, Tabori & Chang
An imprint of ABRAMS

Library of Congress Control Number: 2013935990

ISBN: 978-1-61769-034-1
Target ISBN: 978-1-61769-092-1

Editor: Jennifer Levesque
Designer: Amy Sly
Production Manager: Erin Vandeveer

The text of this book was composed in Sentinel and Avenir.

Printed and bound in the United States

10 9 8 7 6 5 4 3 2

Stewart, Tabori & Chang books are available at special discounts when purchased in quantity for premiums and promotions as well as fundraising or educational use. Special editions can also be created to specification. For details, contact specialsales@abramsbooks.com or the address below.

# ABRAMS

THE ART OF BOOKS SINCE 1949

115 West 18th Street
New York, NY 10011
www.abramsbooks.com

# CONTENTS

This book is dedicated
to my amazing daughters,
Poet and Jagger, and to
my incredible husband
for turning every day into
a party!

# Introduction

I love to throw parties. Any chance I get to celebrate puts me over the moon. Every part of the process is fun and exciting to me. Even if I'm in the midst of total chaos, I find the fun in pulling it all together. I take pride in coming up with unique ideas. And the best part? My kids have become little party planners along with me! We think of concepts together and then bring them to life as a family.

Often, my husband looks at me like I'm crazy, and sometimes I'm convinced he thinks I've totally lost it. Bigger balloons, more color, let's step back into the eighties, a luau on the beach, or a safari. My husband has lived through every out-there idea I've come up with. The truth is I just love celebrating. I can't help myself! When I was a kid, my mom always made our birthdays special. We loved doing themed parties and coming up with creative ideas together. This is one of the reasons I enjoy carrying on the tradition so much. Celebrations don't have to be saved for special occasions; every day we can make something special happen.

I also understand the stresses that can go along with throwing a great party. Planning can be hard, finding the time to do everything you need to do can be challenging, and too much stress can turn good family fun into a tense situation fast. I love to cook, but I usually have only about fifteen minutes to throw something together. Keeping things on a budget can also be an issue; I find so much joy in my kids' being happy with their birthdays, but I don't want to spend a fortune putting them together. I want everything to be stunning but also totally affordable. And the planning process needs to fit into my schedule as a busy mom. At the end of the day, I want to put together something truly special but also for it to be accessible, easy to pull off, and most important, fun.

So after spending years coming up with fun ways to celebrate our family get-togethers, I decided I had to put it into a book. The book I wish I'd had. A book that would serve as an inspiration board for me, my family, friends, and other parents looking for fantastic party ideas for their little ones. In this party-planning book, you will find inspiration for more than twenty parties, including a movie night, a pirate party, a spa day, a baseball party, and many more. Each party includes crafts and recipes you and your children can make together that are both easy and affordable. You will also find a reference guide in the last chapter that highlights some of the places, both online and off-line, where I find my party essentials.

I don't know about you, but half the time I find myself staring at a recipe, trying to figure it out. Or struggling over a blog post that makes home decor look easy, but when I try it myself, it makes me feel like I must be crazy. Did everyone else go to the Martha Stewart Academy? And why didn't I get the invite to sign up? This book is meant to be a beautiful but simple guide that will inspire you to take matters into your own hands and create a magical world for your family to indulge in. Whether you've been crafting for years, are the best baker on the block, or it's your first time throwing a kids' party, this book is for you. It's meant for everyone, and it's designed to be fun for the whole family.

**Now let's get ready to party!**

# Carnival & Circus, Oh My!

One of my favorite ideas for this book was a carnival theme. I couldn't wait to try it out in my own house. The party was so much fun! We had a ring toss game, a beanbag throw, bobbing for apples, and circus-inspired food. Once we put this all together at our house, it was a blast. It's an awesome, fun, and affordable party idea, and it's easy to let the kids be part of the process. The kids had a great time with the games, and my friend even sewed together little beanbags for the beanbag toss. We used cans from our pantry as the target and turned it into a party. Other ideas for this party could include different stands for carnival goodies like popcorn, cotton candy, and snow cones. Need more games? Try your own variation of a fishbowl toss.

# WHITE CHOCOLATE–DIPPED STRAWBERRIES

Chocolate-covered strawberries are so yummy, and making them festive can be fun for the kids as well as easy. My daughter Jagger had such a blast with the red sprinkles. And they can be a great addition to carnival-inspired food or candy.

### YIELD: 12 STRAWBERRIES

Parchment paper

1 cup of white chocolate chips

12 large strawberries

Red sugar sprinkles

Cover a tray with parchment paper. Heat white chocolate chips on low heat, stirring constantly. Once the chips have melted into a smooth consistency, remove from heat. Poke the stem end of a strawberry with a fork, and dip into the melted chips. Place on parchment paper and sprinkle with red sugar sprinkles. Repeat for remaining strawberries. Refrigerate or let chocolate coating firm before serving.

# BEANBAG TOSS

A beanbag toss is such a classic game to include in any carnival. My friend's homemade beanbags were a big hit! They had felt initials sewed on and were adorable. This game was a favorite with the kids during our party.

3 to 6 cans
3 beanbags

Grab cans out of your cupboard, remove labels if desired, and stack in a pyramid. For a small pyramid use three cans; for a larger pyramid use six cans and stack them. Have players stand back at a marked distance and give them each three beanbags for three chances to knock down as many cans as they can.

# RING TOSS GAME

What's a circus carnival without a ring toss? I have great memories of going to the carnival as a kid. Whenever we traveled, my mom would take me to the nearest carnival or fair as soon as we got to our destination. I always loved the ring toss game.

8 colored soda bottles

Sand

Crate

1 ring per kid (see "How to Make the Rings")

Masking tape

Place bottles randomly inside the crate. If you use empty soda bottles, fill them halfway with sand so they won't get tipped over. Give each child a ring and three chances to get the ring around a bottle. Use a piece of masking tape on the floor to show the kids where to stand. Younger children can stand closer.

## HOW TO MAKE THE RINGS

1 wood embroidery hoop per kid

½ roll of glitter ribbon per ring

1 pair of scissors

Unscrew the hoop to loosen the outside ring from the inner ring. Slide one end of the ribbon between the two rings to secure. Now have each player wrap the ribbon around the outside to cover the wood with the circus-friendly glimmer. When the entire hoop is covered in ribbon, cut the end of the ribbon, slide the remaining end between the two rings, and tighten the screw. Now the kids will be ready for the ring toss game.

# BOBBING FOR APPLES

I had forgotten how much fun I used to have bobbing for apples until I saw the kids doing it. It's easy and fun for all ages. Don't forget to keep some towels nearby to dry off all the wet little faces.

1 large bucket

Water

6 to 8 apples

Fill the bucket three-quarters full with water. Place the apples in the water and have each player try to pick one up with their teeth. Remember, hands behind the back!

=== TIPS ===

- Red and white make a great color theme for the carnival.

- Tie balloons with twine instead of ribbon to create a vintage feeling.

- Think outside the box when it comes to music and decorations. The kids started break dancing in the middle of the party, and right away it felt like a real carnival.

- Reintroduce classic games in a fun way to give your party a unique flair.

# Spa La La

A great party to put together is a mini spa for your little ones. One summer day we brought the kids together, made lemonade, broke out the nail polish, and sliced cucumbers for a spa afternoon. They put on their favorite music, and it cost us very little money to create super-fun memories. The kids did one another's fingernails and toenails, made lemonade, and lounged around with cucumber slices on their eyes. They felt like real-life princesses. This is one of my favorite inexpensive parties to do. Other ideas for spa day include fruit-infused water, homemade facials, and of course a selection of kid-friendly books.

# PINK LEMONADE

Homemade lemonade is fun to make for the family. The kids loved being a part of mixing the ingredients.

### YIELD: 8–10 SERVINGS

2 cups lemon juice, freshly squeezed (about 12 to 14 lemons)

1 cup sugar

3 tablespoons grenadine

7 cups cold water

Lemon slices for garnish

Ice

Fill a pitcher with the freshly squeezed lemon juice and add sugar, grenadine, and water. Mix well and top with ice. Garnish each glass with a lemon slice. We usually like our pink lemonade tart, but if your kids prefer it sweeter, just add more sugar.

# SUGAR SCRUB

Make a natural sugar scrub that your kids will love. Not only will everyone leave with skin feeling soft and smooth, but all the ingredients can be found in your kitchen. Nothing like a craft that will make both parents and kids happy.

½ cup raw sugar per scrub

¼ cup almond oil per scrub

1 jar per kid

1 Popsicle stick per kid

1 glass dropper per scented oil

6 to 8 drops of essential oils per scrub

Have each kid mix together the sugar and almond oil in his or her jar, using a Popsicle stick. To create a consistency to your liking, add more oil to make it smoother, or more sugar to create a more exfoliating mixture. Have the kids use a glass dropper to stir in their combination of essential oils for fragrance. Mix well.

# PERFUME

Calming scents are an amazing addition to any spa party, but it's even better when you get to combine your favorite scents to make your own perfume. Making your own fragrance is a personal, fun, and creative experience that the kids will love. Encourage even more creativity by having each kid name his or her own perfume—"coconut creation" was one of our favorites.

2 teaspoons jojoba oil per fragrance (almond oil may be substituted)

10 to 12 drops essential oil(s) per fragrance

1 glass dropper per scented oil

1 vial (with cork) per kid

Allow each child to use a glass dropper to add the jojoba or almond oil to his or her vial. Next, have the kids add their combinations of essential oils to the vials. Great essential oils to work with are lavender, vanilla, mint, coconut, and lemon. Some of these oils can even be found in your pantry in the form of extracts. Add 5 to 6 drops of essential oil scents for every teaspoon of jojoba oil. Cork, and shake for 2 minutes. As the fragrance matures, the aromas will blend together even more to create a stronger scent. Test first to make sure that your little one's skin is not too sensitive to the scents. To test, add 1 drop to the forearm and wait for 1 hour to make sure no irritation has occurred. Experiment, and remember to have fun!

# NAIL PAINTING/RELAXATION

Get the kids together and pick out their favorite nail polish colors. They can make patterns or designs and take turns doing one another's nails. They can slice cucumbers to put on their eyes and make a playlist together that they can listen to while they enjoy their spa time. The girls loved picking out their favorite songs during the spa day and learning about new songs from their friends. Play the tunes, drink some lemonade, and let the relaxation begin.

=== TIPS ===

- You can create great labels for your perfumes and scrubs with stylish tape.

- Take the kids to the farmers' market to pick out fresh fruit to eat during their spa day. Here's a picture I took with my kids at our local farmers' market.

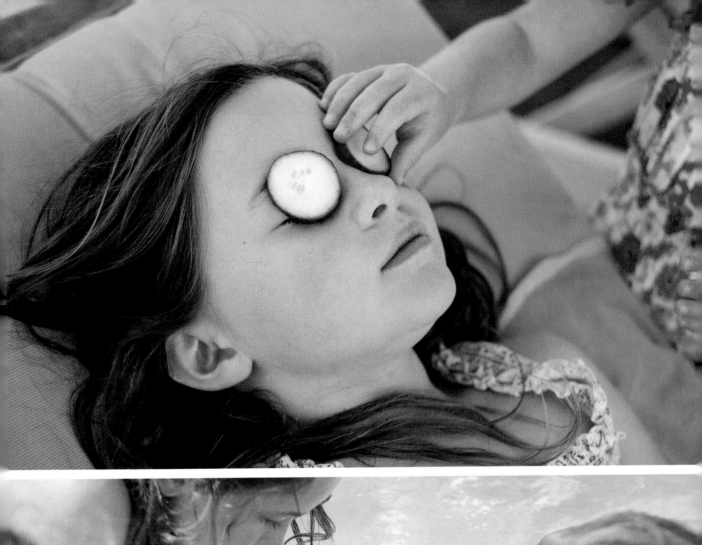

# Pirate's Life for Me

A pirate party is a great theme. Costumes are easy to make, and the possibilities for games and favors are endless. It might sound like something boys would enjoy more than girls, but it's amazing how universal rocking out on the high seas can be. My good friend Jenni had an amazing pirate birthday party for her son, and I was surprised to see how much my daughters loved it! Some other fun ideas include "message in a bottle"–inspired invitations, and pirate-themed snack names.

# BUCCANEER ROOT BEER FLOATS

Turn this classic childhood drink into an awesome pirate treat. With scoops of ice cream foaming the mug, the little pirates will be both surprised and excited for their buccaneer floats. So gather the ingredients and get ready for this easy and quick recipe.

**YIELD: 1 SERVING**

1 mug per kid

1 to 2 cups root beer, chilled

1 to 2 scoops vanilla ice cream per float

Fill each mug half full with root beer. Slowly add scoops of vanilla ice cream. Top with root beer until full. Make sure to add the root beer slowly, as it will foam over the sides if added too fast. Encourage slurping, mug clinking, and lots of pirate songs.

# TREASURE DIG

Dig for the buried treasure with this awesome game! This is what we thought of as an alternative to the treasure hunt. Who knew a bucket, sand, and treasures could go such a long way?

Place some treasures at the bottom of a barrel. Fill the barrel a third of the way with sand, hide more treasures, and fill it another third of the way. One by one, blindfold your pirates, give them each a small rake or shovel, and give them thirty seconds apiece to dig for treasure. Whatever they find, they get to keep.

=== TIPS ===

- There are so many ways to recycle what you have in your house. The spyglasses made from paper towel inserts and the hats made of newspaper helped make our party so great (see next page). Oftentimes we think we have to spend money to create something magical for our kids when so many of these things are already in our home.

- I am so lucky to be Target's Mommy Ambassador. Before I started working with them, I was the mom who spent hours in the aisles. I still do. We got our eye patches and treasures from Target. You can also go to Target.com to find lots of goodies!

# SPYGLASSES AND HATS

Pirates definitely need their spyglasses to keep an eye out for ships on the horizon. So save those cardboard paper towel inserts, and make this project an eco-friendly craft that the kids will love. Once the little buccaneers are ready to climb the crow's nest and head out to sea, they need one last pirate accessory: hats, of course! Get ready for these fun crafts to create a pirate day filled with adventure.

1 paper towel insert per kid

2 tablespoons each of red, black, and white paint

1 paintbrush for each color

1 sheet of newspaper per kid

Glitter, plastic jewels, ribbon (optional)

Give each child a paper towel insert for his or her "spyglass." Lay out a pirate's array of paint colors—red, black, and white—and have the kids paint their spyglasses. For fancier spyglasses, they can add glitter, plastic jewels, or ribbons.

Follow these easy instructions for making your pirate hat: Take a sheet of newspaper and fold it in half from top to bottom. Place the folded sheet horizontally and fold down both corners so they meet in the middle. You'll notice there are two flaps at the bottom. Take one flap and fold it in half and then in half again. Turn the hat over and fold up the other flap the same way. Now your hat is ready for the high seas!

# TREASURE CHESTS

All pirates need their own treasure chests. This was a favorite for the kids. Who wouldn't like a personalized treasure chest to take home as a keepsake? Treasures and all . . .

1 piece of "aged" paper per kid

1 unpainted wooden chest per kid

2 tablespoons each of various paint colors

1 paintbrush for each color

1 sheet of stickers for each kid

1 cup of sand per chest

4 to 6 trinkets per chest

To "age" the paper, gently run a flame along the edges of each sheet. Make sure to do this safely before the kids arrive. This is best done over a sink to prevent accidents. Let each little pirate choose a wooden chest, and have them start decorating with paints and stickers. Next, have them write their own pirate message on the paper, and roll it up to form a scroll. Lay out sand and an array of trinkets for the kids to fill up their treasure chests. It will surely be a hit!

# Love, Love, Love

I love Valentine's Day. What's not to love about a holiday that celebrates love? But there are great ways to celebrate beyond the typical cards, flowers, and chocolate hearts. Every year, my brother and his awesome wife, Ilse, put together a Valentine's scavenger hunt for the kids. They put an incredible amount of time and thought into creating fun, challenging adventures that get better every year. So far, we've done a neighborhood expedition, a sandy beach journey, and an amazing race all over the city. My brother and his wife create clues and plant them along the scavenger hunt's path, and I get to lead the kids on the hunt! Here are some fun ideas for celebrating Valentine's Day with the ones you love.

# SANDY'S SUGAR COOKIES

My friend Lisa gave me a delicious family recipe from Grandma Sandy. I could eat an entire batch of these cookies by myself!

**YIELD: 3 DOZEN COOKIES**

**CREAM TOGETHER**
2 cups sugar

3 eggs

1 cup softened butter

2 teaspoons vanilla extract

**ADD AND MIX WELL**
4 cups flour

¾ teaspoon baking powder

¼ teaspoon salt

Cream together the sugar, eggs, softened butter, and vanilla extract. Then add the flour, baking powder, and salt, and mix well. Cover the mixed dough with plastic wrap and chill for 1 hour. Roll out the chilled dough to about ¼-inch thickness, and use cookie cutters to cut desired shapes. Place on ungreased baking sheets, leaving at least ½ inch between cookies. Bake at 375°F for about 10 minutes or until golden brown.

## CONFECTIONER'S ICING

Add about 2 tablespoons of milk or water to 2 cups of confectioner's sugar (10X powdered) to make a desired spreading consistency. Add a dash of salt and a teaspoon of vanilla extract, to taste. Add food-coloring drops, if desired.

# BOX OF LOVE

We all love getting a Valentine's Day card, but it's also fun to create a whole box full of love filled with hearts and treats! This is a great craft to do for moms, dads, grandparents, and even siblings. The box will serve as a reminder of how special they are all year long.

1 cardboard box, heart shaped or square (can be found at most craft stores), per kid

1 sheet of stickers per kid

Selection of markers for crafts

1 sheet of colored paper per box

1 teaspoon of confetti per box

3 or 4 heart cutouts

2 to 4 Hershey's Kisses or other favorite candy per box

Have each child decorate the outside of his or her box with stickers and markers. Next, have the kids write a note, draw a picture, or add a special message on the colored paper to roll up and place inside the box. Add confetti, heart cutouts, and candy for an extra touch of love. When everything is done, give the box to someone special and see how loved it makes them feel.

# HEART WANDS

This was one of the crafts that I was really looking forward to doing with the girls. They love wands, hearts, and everything valentine related, so I figured this would be a hit for the holiday . . . and I was right. They loved working together on this project.

1 (9 x 12") sheet of felt per kid

1 bottle tacky glue

1 bag of fiberfill stuffing

1 (½ x 12") wood dowel per heart

8 to 10 mini clothespins per heart

2 pairs scissors

Holding two pieces of felt together, use scissors to cut out hearts. A standard sheet should give you room to create two hearts side by side. Using the double-sheet method will make your hearts the same size and shape, which is important for your wand. Glue the two heart pieces together along the edges, making sure to leave an inch-wide opening at the top and bottom so you can add the stuffing later. Let the glue dry completely—overnight is best. If you've got impatient little ones and need a shorter wait time, use mini clothespins to keep the heart pieces together while you add the stuffing. Insert a dowel at the bottom of the heart to make the wand, and finish gluing the top and bottom together.

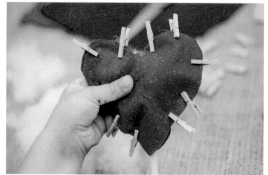

# SCAVENGER HUNT

First, decide which kind of scavenger hunt suits your family best. If you have little ones, you might want to stick to a short route in your own neighborhood that can be traveled easily on foot or by bike. For bigger kids, hop in the car and head out on the town! We've used all kinds of hiding places in our scavenger hunts: inside libraries, behind street signs, in trees, and buried in the dirt. We love using riddles that the kids need to figure out before they can find the clue. The older they get, the more complicated the riddles can be. Make it creative and challenging enough to be fun, but not so obscure that anyone gets frustrated. The goal is to have a blast! At the end of our hunts, we always have a little Valentine's Day surprise for everyone.

One year we went to a cupcake shop where our first clue was hidden in a cupcake box. When the kids opened the box, there were cupcakes for each kid and a letter that included a word scramble that spelled out where to go next. We also did fill-in-the-blank puzzles and guessing games. Usually we have six to eight clues—one for each part of the hunt before the final destination. For simpler scavenger hunts, I hide handmade cards in the backyard and have the kids find them to discover what adventures we are going on. It makes for a great day that your kids will always remember.

## TIPS

- Rubber-stamping a heart or cupid on goodies from the kitchen or placing a hangtag on a vase with flowers can inspire you to turn any household item into a little valentine for a loved one.

- Take your kids to the local farmers' market or flower market, then decorate the house with beautiful flowers.

- Decorating the house can be super-fun and festive. Let the little ones get involved by adding their personal touches, like a Valentine's Day drawing for Mom or Dad or a batch of homemade cookies in the shape of hearts.

- We include new and fun ideas all the time on Moonfrye.com, so come check it out for inspiration.

# Wild Safari Adventure

A safari adventure is a great unisex party. We had a few friends come over, and the kids had a blast. Both the boys and the girls got super into it. We had a mini safari and made binoculars to complete the search. The binoculars were made out of toilet paper cardboard inserts and were adorable. As I've mentioned, I love recycling and reusing. It teaches our kids about the planet and encourages creative play! Other ideas for a safari party include animal face painting and safari-inspired snacks like animal crackers and banana chips.

# ICE-CREAM SHAKE

This safari-themed recipe makes a yummy ice-cream shake that kids and parents will love. Get creative by adding the kids' favorite gooey toppings, and have fun with it.

**YIELD: 2 SERVINGS**

2 cups mint chip ice cream (or your child's favorite ice cream)

½ cup milk, or less

2 Oreo cookies

1 graham cracker, crumbled (optional)

Use a blender to combine the ice cream, milk, and cookies until the consistency is smooth. For a thicker milkshake, use less milk. Sprinkle graham crackers on top, if desired, and serve in a chilled glass with a straw.

# BINOCULARS

Field binoculars are standard issue for any safari adventure. How else are you supposed to spot all the animals? So grab some household items, and let's get this adventure started.

2 toilet paper cardboard inserts (or 1 paper towel insert cut in half) per kid

2 tablespoons each of various paint colors

1 paintbrush per color

1 (15- to 20-inch) leather string per kid

1 hole punch for crafts

1 bottle nontoxic glue

Have the children paint the cardboard inserts any way they would like. Let them use a wide array of colors—creative play is the name of the game. Once the masterpieces have dried, glue the two pieces together, side by side. Using a hole punch, create a hole on the outer side of each cardboard insert in order to attach the leather string. Just feed the ends of the leather string through each hole and knot inside. Next up? Wildlife safari!

# ANIMAL MASKS

Turn safari-goers into the animals of their choice. From tigers to bears, the possibilities are endless. It's a fun way to engage the adventurers and ignite their creativity.

1 animal mask per kid

Selection of paints and brushes

1 pair of scissors

Pick up animal masks from a local craft store, or trace and cut out your own using thin cardboard or poster board. Have each kid think of an animal and paint their rendition of it. It can even be a made-up animal. Most masks will come with elastic bands. If you make your own, pick up some elastic from the craft store and attach the ends to each side of the mask.

# SAFARI ADVENTURE

Scavenger hunt meets hide-and-seek! Hide animal figures around the backyard, and have the kids go on a safari adventure to find them. You can reuse animal figures that your kids may already have, or purchase new ones at a local toy store. It's also worth checking out local thrift stores for treasures. A fun way to end the hunt is to play a variation of charades in which the kids act out the animals they've found, and everyone has to guess which animal they are portraying. Guaranteed to keep everyone guessing—and laughing—until all the animals, real and make-believe, have had their turn in the spotlight.

=== TIPS ===

- Create a super-cute safari station that includes your favorite animal-shaped gummy candies.

- Make cute signs to put up at the different stations of the party. Hand-painted signs are an easy way to make your party look authentic. You and your kids can create cute names that have adventure themes like "Rainforest Exploration" or "Wildlife Reserve."

# Spring Is in the Air

Spring is one of my favorite times of year. We spend lots of time in our yard, reading and doing crafts. The girls also love doing fairy hunts in the spring. We walk through our neighborhood and try to get to the beach if we can. For the past few years it has rained on Jagger's birthday, which is in the spring, but usually it is sunny skies here in California. It is the perfect time for a little gathering with the kids. For this party, I've included an easy watermelon pops recipe, an eggshell flower craft, and a fun-filled balloon relay race for a spring-inspired day.

# WATERMELON POPS

We love watermelon, and it is a yummy and healthy treat for our kids. Spring is the perfect opportunity to bring out the fresh watermelon. The girls love these unique pops because it is a totally new way to eat the fruit they love.

### YIELD: 8–10 SERVINGS

1 large watermelon

20 Popsicle sticks

Ice

Bucket

Cut 2-inch-thick slices of watermelon, and then cut each slice into triangular quarters. Make a small cut in the middle of the green rind of each piece, and insert a Popsicle stick. When you're ready to serve, lay the pops on a bed of ice in a bucket for the kids to eat cold.

# FLORAL EGGSHELLS

This is an awesome craft because you can use items around the house or outside. As a family, we always love to find ways to reuse and recycle. Preparing for this party, we cooked scrambled eggs for breakfast, saved the shells, and then cleaned them out for this special craft.

1 egg per kid

2 to 4 pinches of soil per egg

2 or 3 flowers and pieces of greenery per egg

1 or 2 pinches of moss per egg

When you crack the egg, make sure you tap only the tip on the side of the sink and pull apart the top of the shell so the bottom stays intact. Rinse and let dry. If there are any jagged pieces, break them off so it's not as sharp. Have each child place some soil in the bottom of the egg. Clip flowers and greenery for each child to create his or her own arrangement. Place moss around the flowers for an extra spring-y look.

# BALLOON-AND-SPOON RACE

This balloon race is much easier to clean up than the traditional egg-and-spoon race. First, create an obstacle course that the kids go through—this can be as simple or as complex as you want. Each player stands behind the starting line with a filled water balloon balanced on a spoon. Start the race by counting down or blowing a whistle. All players must go as fast as they can while balancing their balloons. Any player who drops the balloon must get a new one and start over. The first player who succeeds in balancing the balloon all the way through the obstacle course wins. Remember to tell the kids that their hands can be used only to hold the spoon. It was incredible to see how much fun kids can have with just water balloons and spoons. And when it turned into a water fight, it reminded me of hot days from my own childhood. Seeing all the kids working together was adorable and proved to us that kids need very little to have a good time.

## TIPS

- Whenever possible, use things that you already have accessible. We had a blast doing the eggshell craft, and all of the supplies were found in and around our home. We used eggs from the refrigerator and fresh flowers and soil from our yard.

- Simplicity is often key. Taking fresh fruit and turning it into pops or making classic lemonade and putting it in a beautiful bottle is a way to liven up any party and keep it on a budget.

CHAPTER
7

# It's Slumber Time

When I sat down to write this chapter on slumber parties, it brought back so many amazing memories. My mom used to make one giant bed out of sleeping bags on the floor, and I would put all my teddy bears around me. We would sleep in my big brother's room. We would call our house "Camp Soleil" because so many friends were in and out of it. Now when my girls have a friend stay over, it's such fun to see their eyes light up playing games, telling each other stories, and getting the giggles when it's time to turn off the lights. I love to see them truly living in the moment.

# PERSONALIZED PILLOWCASES

This craft will make the kids happy long after the slumber party ends. Every child gets to go home with a pillowcase to remember his or her night full of fun.

Craft paper

1 pillowcase per kid

1 piece of wax paper per pillowcase

2 tablespoons each of various fabric paint colors (adjust amount for multiple kids)

1 paintbrush per color

This could get a little messy, so lay out craft paper to catch any spills. Put a piece of wax paper inside of each pillowcase to prevent the paint from leaking through. Set up an array of paints for the kids to choose from, and let them paint their hearts away. If they want to paint both sides of the pillowcase, let the first side dry completely before painting the other side. Have the kids take their pillowcases home in the morning.

# FROOT LOOP NECKLACES

What kid won't like jewelry they can eat? Froot Loops are not only yummy, they're also the perfect shape for this craft.

1 (20-inch) string per kid

1 large box Froot Loops cereal

1 large bowl

On each piece of string, tie a triple knot 2 inches from the top. This leaves enough room to tie the ends together after the necklace is made. Make sure all the kids' hands are washed and clean. Put out a bowl of Froot Loops, and the kids will be eager to do the rest. Have them put on the Froot Loops in their favorite order. Once the necklace is full, tie a knot at the end and then tie the two ends together, and let the kids enjoy their new jewelry they can eat!

# GAME NIGHT

Grab your kids' favorite games and make it one of those nights! Twister, charades, and Scrabble are some of our household favorites. Put out a selection, and have the kids pick their favorite. Board game nights are a perfect opportunity to bond with the kids and create lasting memories.

# BOX-FLIP DARE

Truth or dare was always a favorite when I was growing up, so we came up with a kid-friendly version. Create your very own box-flip dare game!

1 (4-inch-square) folded box

2 tablespoons each of 6 paint colors

1 paintbrush per color

Selection of markers for decorating

It is great to work side by side with your little ones. Help your child fold the box and choose different color paints for each side. While the paint dries, come up with "dares": "Act like a gorilla," "Tell us a secret," "Pick someone to have a stare contest with," "Sing your favorite song," "Do a cartwheel." I am sure the kids will have their own ideas. The finished product is a unique box full of fun-to-be moments. Have each child take a turn tossing the box up in the air, and whatever it says on the side it lands on, it is their turn to do.

## TIPS

- Add style to your slumber party. Take raffia and natural-looking spoons and tie them around colorful mini cereal boxes for the next morning's breakfast.

- Pick out some movie classics, and pass out the popcorn for a fun nostalgia night.

- Karaoke is a great way to add some spunk to your party.

- Why wait? Have the kids show up in their favorite PJs.

# PANCAKES

Nothing tops homemade pancakes the morning after a slumber party. Well, nothing except for this amazing pancake bar with toppings sure to make every kid happy.

### YIELD: 10–12 PANCAKES

1 cup all-purpose flour

1 tablespoon white sugar

1 teaspoon baking powder

½ teaspoon baking soda

½ teaspoon salt

¾ cup milk

1 egg

2 tablespoons butter, melted

½ teaspoon vanilla extract

**TOPPINGS**
Sliced strawberries

Blueberries

Sliced bananas

Chocolate chips

Sprinkles

Maple syrup

In a large bowl, mix together the dry ingredients. Pour in the milk, egg, melted butter, and vanilla extract. Mix until smooth. Heat a lightly oiled frying pan on medium heat. Pour the batter into the pan a large spoonful at a time and cook until bubbles begin to form. Then flip, cooking until lightly browned on both sides. Let the pancakes cool and bring out the cookie cutters for a fun pancake bar. Place the fresh fruit and other toppings in bowls and set them out to serve.

# CHAPTER 8

# A Sparkling Fourth of July

The Fourth of July is one of our favorite holidays. I have always wanted to go to Martha's Vineyard to have a truly East Coast experience. I wanted to literally walk around wearing red, white, and blue. I have family and friends across the country who really get into the holiday, and being there brought me back to my roots. It was incredible to see how people truly celebrate. For this party, get ready for an amazing corn-on-the-cob recipe with a fun bunting craft that's perfect for the Independence Day holiday.

# CORN ON THE COB

I love going to a restaurant called Café Habana. I used to go to the one in New York City, and then our friends Kelly and Jamie introduced us to the one in Malibu. This recipe is inspired by my love of the corn there. I tried to re-create the taste to the best of my ability. My kids love spices, but if your kids are not into spicy foods, this recipe can be altered to taste just as delicious.

## YIELD: 4 SERVINGS

4 ears corn

¼ cup mayonnaise

2 tablespoons sour cream

¼ teaspoon cumin

1 pinch of salt

1 tablespoon butter

1 cup cotija cheese

**FOR THE SPICE LOVERS**
1 pinch of cayenne pepper
(optional)

Before baking, peel off the husk of each ear of corn. Place the corn in a pan and bake at 350°F for 30 to 40 minutes. Mix together the mayonnaise, sour cream, cumin, and salt and set aside. While the corn is hot, place corn holders on the ends of each ear and rub the corn with butter. Next, slather on the mayonnaise mixture. Crumble the cotija cheese onto the coated corn, and season with the cayenne pepper. If your little ones aren't fans of spiciness, no worries—leave out the spices. This is one of our favorite additions to dinner!

# ANTIQUED BUNTING

This bunting helps create a classic vintage feeling for your Independence Day celebration.

Water

Large pot

1 pair tongs

Bunting fabric

10 to 15 black-tea bags

Boil water, and remove from heat. Using tongs, place the bunting fabric into the hot water. Add 10 or more tea bags, depending on how antiqued you want your bunting to be. Let the fabric soak until it's the desired color, and then hang it to dry. When you're done, pick a location to hang your new decoration.

# BBQ & SPARKLERS

What's more fun than the family getting together for a barbecue? I recently discovered that my husband makes amazing food on the grill. I love that it took only sixteen years to figure this out. It was a really fun bonding experience for the family, and we ended our family barbecue by lighting sparklers. When I was a kid, my family would go down to the beach on the Fourth of July to light sparklers, so this activity really brought back memories for me.

═══════════════ TIPS ═══════════════

- You can add a festive umbrella to your drink. Stick the umbrella in a piece of lemon or orange so that it stays in place.

- If you are planning on being outdoors, don't forget your citronella candles to ward off insects and avoid bites.

# A Luau Full of Alohas

Since we have little ones, we are always trying to come up with ideas for creative play. The kids are constantly active and discovering new and inspired ways to celebrate. It is something we strive for. We want to encourage their imaginations, have a great time, create magical experiences with them, and, at the same time, keep it within our budget. Over the summer we came up with a super-fun party idea that was easy to do at the last minute and found ourselves having a luau on the beach at five p.m. on a Friday.

# PINEAPPLE SPRITZER

Luaus are great for making kid-friendly drinks. Make it fun by adding slices of pineapple or another tropical fruit to your drinks. The kids will love adding their own tropical touches. To make it even more tropical, try serving your drinks right out of coconuts or pineapples.

### YIELD: 6 SERVINGS

32 mint leaves

2 large oranges, halved

½ cup simple syrup (equal parts white sugar and water)

½ cup pineapple juice

4 cups sparkling water

Ice

Put the mint leaves into a glass pitcher and squeeze the orange halves over them. Muddle the mint using the end of a wooden spoon. In a saucepan, combine the sugar and water. Heat and stir until the sugar has dissolved. Let cool, then add the simple syrup and pineapple juice. Top with sparkling water and serve over ice.

# SEASHELL CANDLES

This is one of my favorite projects in the whole book. I was super-excited to make homemade candles and found myself trying to turn almost anything I had into a candle. I felt the urge to make my entire house into a candle factory. The kids can get involved too by decorating and packaging their candles as gifts. As the wax is cooling down, they can pick out decorations like small seashells and sand.

**HERE'S WHAT YOU'LL NEED**

1 oyster seashell per kid

4 tablespoons chopped wax per shell

1 empty, clean can, such as a soup can

6 cups water

1 pair tongs

1 wick and wick holder per shell

Heat-resistant gloves

Crayons (optional)

Make sure all of the seashells are clean and dry. Place the chopped wax into the can. You can save soup cans and even re-cycle your old candles for wax. Boil water and, using the tongs, place the can halfway into the water. Wait 3 to 5 minutes for the wax to melt. Place the wick with its holder into the seashell. Using gloves, pour the melted wax into the seashells until they are three-quarters full. The wax should harden in 20 to 30 minutes. If you're feeling even more crafty, add bits of crayons to the melting wax to create pops of color. Be very careful while making the candles. As I discovered, wax can be very hot.

# 'ULU MAIKA HAWAIIAN BOWLING GAME

'Ulu maika is an ancient Hawaiian game that resembles bowling. It's easy to play and is great for any age, toddler to adult! Normally it's played using a round disk, but what could be more festive than a coconut?

2 wooden stakes

2 coconuts

Place two wooden stakes in the ground 2 feet apart. You can make the game more or less challenging by changing the distance between the stakes. Take a coconut, and bowl away.

## TIPS

- To add some authenticity to your luau, use mini umbrellas to skewer the fruit. It looks festive, and kids have a blast eating the fruit. Just be careful of the skewer's pointy ends.

- Candles make wonderful homemade gifts. Since presentation is key, make the wrapping unique by adding natural elements such as a craft box, recycled shred, and twine.

# Enchanted Midsummer Dream

I love co-ed parties. Imaginations run wild when boys and girls get together. It's so much fun to see the games and pretend scenarios they come up with. This is a great way to do a party that both the boys and girls in your life will enjoy. Bring everyone together for a midsummer princesses-and-knights party. One weekend, we threw an impromptu princesses-and-knights party, and the kids had an absolute blast. The boys decorated shields, and the girls made crowns. It was fantastic!

# MIDSUMMER SHAPED SANDWICHES

With so many food allergies to be aware of, we try to avoid serving peanuts when we're entertaining. My husband is allergic, so I have learned the hard way. For this medieval-inspired snack, we used almond butter instead of peanut butter. It's a nice option that's safe for peanut-allergic kids and still tastes delicious. Add a little style to your party with custom hangtags identifying sandwich names and saying what is inside them.

**YIELD: 2 SANDWICHES**

Large cookie cutters

2 slices white bread

2 slices wheat bread

2 tablespoons whipped cream cheese

4 slices cucumber

2 tablespoons almond butter

1 tablespoon jelly

Using cookie cutters, cut bread into shapes. We love to mix and match different types of bread for flavor, so we included both white and wheat breads. Fill one sandwich with cucumber slices and cream cheese and another with almond butter and jelly. Feeling crazy? Name them something wild for a fun snack worthy of any princess or knight.

# FAIRY HOMES

One of our favorite at-home activities is making gifts for fairies. My girls love leaving treasures and notes in the backyard for their "fairies" to find. This is a great way to make homes for these precious little visitors.

1 egg per kid

2 tablespoons glitter per egg

2 to 4 flowers per egg

1 piece of paper per egg

Crack just the top of an egg, leaving the majority of the shell intact. Carefully remove the top third of the eggshell and rinse the remaining portion. Let each shell dry completely. When the eggshell is dry, pour glitter inside and surround with flowers to make a nest. Have the kids write special notes to their fairies, then roll the notes up and place them inside their fairy home. Now you have the perfect home for fairies!

# FLOWER CROWNS

We loved this theme, and the kids were looking forward to it. Crafting at this party was such a fun and creative experience. We wanted to create something whimsical for the girls, and this was the perfect choice.

- 1 (16- to 20-inch) piece of wired twine per kid
- 4 to 6 flowers per crown
- 2 or 3 twist ties per crown
- 4 to 6 (8-inch) lengths of ribbon per crown
- 1 pair craft scissors

Mold each piece of wired twine into a circle that fits comfortably around each princess's head. If you buy precut twine, you may need two pieces to achieve this. Once you have the right size, double-wrap any extra twine around the circle. Have the princesses pick and cut the flowers they want to use. Place each flower in the desired position and secure using a twist tie. Continue this process until all the flowers are placed on the crown. Finish the crowns by tying on dangling ribbons. This activity is a great one to do with the little ones, but the younger they are, the more help they need.

# SHIELDS

Homemade shields are easy to make with a few items you can find around the home. The boys absolutely loved this craft, and the girls did too!

One large square cardboard box will have four sides to make four shields. Using scissors, slice away each side of the box and then cut it into a shield shape. You can trace your shield onto the cardboard with pencil beforehand, or simply make a V on the bottom edge of each square and cut straight up to the side edges. Next, cut holes into the cardboard on each side and create a handle with a strip of suede, feeding the cord through the holes and tying a knot on the opposite side to secure the handle. Most craft stores have precut suede straps with holes for jewelry making. If you aren't using precut straps, cut 5- to 6-inch pieces and cut one hole at each end. Now the fun part: Have each knight paint and decorate a shield. Use newspaper to prevent spills, and let each shield dry completely before the knights start to play.

# SEARCH FOR GOLD

The medieval knights and princesses go searching for gold in this fun game. Hide little gems and chocolate gold coins throughout the backyard and send them off to find as many pieces as they can. There's nothing like searching for chocolate! The kids are still talking about their search for gold and anticipating the next time they will be able to do it. Some pieces were easier to find than others, but in the end, no chocolate or jewel went unfound. Remember to count the treasures beforehand to make sure no pieces are left behind.

--- TIPS ---

You can create an ethereal place by using your imagination and a little bit of moss. One of my favorite highlights from the party came when my friend Ashley brought over a bunch of real moss and we laid it on a table, creating an enchanted garden. It was beautiful and completed our setup.

# Movie Night

I love going to the movies. Any chance to get to the movies, and I'm there. The kids love movies as well, so what better way to celebrate than with an outdoor movie night for the whole family? It doesn't take much to pull it off—just a projector, a sheet or wall to project onto, some blankets, and your favorite snacks. This is a great way to bring the family together and do something unique and special. It also makes a fun activity year-round that you can change for any season.

# POPCORN STAMPS

You have to put your kettle corn in something, right? Spruce up plain paper bags with an easy stamp. My girls love stamping, and it is a great way for them to express their creativity, so I try to incorporate it into a lot of activities that we do.

1 or 2 plain paper bags per kid

Various rubber stamps

Ink pads

Choose movie-themed stamps like "Popcorn" for the kids to stamp on the bags before filling them. You can also mix in candy, if you're like me and enjoy salty and sweet. Chocolate-covered raisins are my favorite candy to use.

# KETTLE CORN

My friends didn't believe me when I told them how easy it is to make your own kettle corn. We can't decide who likes it more—the kids or the adults. The extra flavor from the dash of salt and the vanilla extract leaves the whole family wanting more . . . and more.

### YIELD: 10 CUPS

¼ cup vegetable oil

¼ cup sugar

¼ teaspoon vanilla extract

½ cup unpopped popcorn kernels

Dash of salt

Place the oil in a large pot and heat carefully over medium heat. Once heated, stir in the sugar, vanilla extract, and popcorn kernels. Cover and shake the pot frequently to coat the kernels as they pop. Once the popping has slowed, remove the pot from the heat, keeping it covered for a minute or so before transferring the popcorn to bowls or bags. Add salt to taste.

# ADMISSION TICKETS

1 paper/hangtag per kid

Selection of colored pencils or markers

Have each kid personalize their own admission ticket! It's a fun way to get them excited about seeing the featured movie and to use their own unique creativity. All you have to do is lay out the hangtags and colored pencils or markers, and they will do the rest. When it comes time to watch the movie, have them turn in their tickets.

# MOVIE OUTDOORS

The best part about an outdoor movie night is the freedom to stretch out and relax. It is so nice to be able to spend time with your loved ones and also talk during the movie without getting in trouble. You can show your favorite holiday movie, make it spooky for a Halloween film, or throw a fun summer screening. We watched home movies at our movie night. Scout out a good location to assemble your movie night. You can project onto a blank wall or a sheet that hangs on a clothesline tied up between two trees (any two structures will do). If you do this indoors, it can be just as special projecting the film onto a wall.

Little touches like adding a tea light to a mason jar filled with popcorn kernels help create a movie ambience for all to enjoy.

# CHAPTER 12

# Under the Stars

Some of my favorite memories of growing up come from when I would sleep under the stars. My mom was a single mom and she raised my brother and me. We had a tiny balcony at one of our first apartments that could fit a sleeping bag. I loved sleeping outside. My mom would make me special treats, and I felt like a queen. As we grew up, our love for sleeping outside continued. My mom had a bed set up in our yard so that we could sleep outside during the summer. Now, as an adult, I jump at any chance to turn our house into a camping adventure. You can set up your camp either inside or outside, depending on your options. It's always fun to turn a bedroom or a living room into a campout site and make it feel like a special experience.

# S'MORES ON A STICK

We had such a blast making these s'mores on a stick, a fun spin on the traditional s'mores our family loves to make. Rather than stacking the graham crackers, marshmallows, and chocolate, kids get to dip and add the amounts to their liking. Changing things up can be so much fun. We used graham crackers to top the chocolate, but you can get creative by adding sprinkles and other favorite toppings. I think I ate as many s'mores as the kids, if not more!

### YIELD: 12 S'MORE STICKS

12 jumbo marshmallows

12 wooden sticks

1 bag chocolate chips

5 graham crackers, crumbled

2 mason jars

Skewer each marshmallow with a wooden stick. Melt the chocolate chips using the double-boiler method: Fill a pot a quarter full of water and bring to a boil. Put the chips inside a smaller pot and place it inside the pot with the boiling water. Stir chocolate frequently and slowly, making sure not to overheat it. Once the chocolate is melted, transfer it to a jar for easy dipping. Crumble the graham crackers using the back of a spoon, and place the crumbs into the other jar. Dip the marshmallow stick into the melted chocolate and then into the graham cracker crumbs. Serve s'mores right away, or place them gently on a plate coated with graham cracker crumbs so they don't stick.

# VOTIVE LANTERNS

This awesome homemade lantern can be used as a night-light when the camping experience is over. I know my girls love doing something creative that they can take home and use, so get prepared for this outdoor-inspired craft.

1 sheet of stickers per kid

1 votive candleholder per kid

2 tablespoons each of various acrylic paint colors

1 paintbrush per color

1 battery-powered LED light per kid

Lay out an array of stickers for the kids to decorate their candle-holders with. Once they have placed their stickers, have them paint their lanterns however they like. Let the paint dry for 30 to 60 minutes, and peel off the stickers. Light will shine out once the lantern is finished and an LED light is placed inside.

# DESIGN A PLANET OR STAR

Teaching our little ones about the planet and the importance of caring for it is very important to me. This craft is the perfect combination of teaching about the solar system and having a creative experience.

1 foam ball (use various sizes) per kid

1 star per kid

1 wooden stick per kid

2 tablespoons each of various paint colors

1 paintbrush per color

1 bottle of nontoxic glue

1 pinch of glitter per kid (optional)

Poke different-sized foam balls onto wooden sticks or glue stars onto wooden sticks. Have each kid create their own planet. Imagination is the key. They can choose whatever paint colors, decorations, and names they want for their planets. They can even sprinkle glitter onto their planet or star for an extra-special touch. Place, stick side down, in a jar, to dry.

# STORY TIME

I went to summer camp every year until I was seventeen years old. I loved it so much and still hold camp close to my heart. It is always fun to sit around a real or imagined campfire. Somehow, campfires usually encourage good discussions, and I love the bonding experience of talking to our little ones around the fire, hearing the incredible things they have to say. Their new favorite line is "Time is going by so fast," and I ask them, "How do you think I feel?"

Every camping trip needs camping stories. Storytelling is the perfect activity to bring out kids' creativity. The kids create their story collectively, adding sentence by sentence until the story is complete. Each kid can add just one sentence or as much as they want to at the time. Continue to go around the circle a certain number of times, or set a time limit per story. This is a perfect way to excite the imagination and make a listening game interactive.

TIPS

- Put out a few musical instruments—cymbals, a banjo, a ukelele—and have the kids create their own camp songs.

- For Poet's summer camp–themed birthday, we stamped a cloth bag for each kid with the word "camp." We filled the bag with marshmallows, graham crackers, and chocolate as a great takeaway for the kids to enjoy later on.

# Picnic Time

Another fun, affordable party to do with the family is an outdoor picnic. I love that it is something you can do through any season. You can make any kind of picnic you want. For girls, we love doing tea parties or pretending we're in Tuscany. For boys, it's fun to do a wilderness picnic or a dinosaur picnic. A great thing to do is to set up a blanket outside or in your home and bring some of their favorite books for reading when they are enjoying their favorite foods. We love reading the classics. One of my favorites is *The Giving Tree*. A picnic is also a nice way to bring back the nostalgia of our own youth, so sack races and homemade crafts are a great addition.

# STRAWBERRY-BANANA YOGURT ICE POPS

When having a picnic at your house, a yummy ice pop is a perfect treat for the kids! These are delicious—and yes, messy, but fun to eat! Be creative and make them your own by using different fruit combinations. Sometimes the fruit mixture doesn't make it to the freezer because my girls are too busy drinking it.

### YIELD: 8–10 POPS

1½ cups French vanilla yogurt

½ cup strawberries, stemmed

1 banana, peeled

2 tablespoons honey

Popsicle sticks

Ice-pop molds or paper cups

Blend the yogurt, fruit, and honey to the consistency your kids like. Divide the mixture into ice-pop molds or paper cups. You can even write your own messages or questions on the Popsicle sticks. Add a stick to each mold or cup. It should stay in place because of the mixture's thick consistency, but if you need a little help getting it to stand straight, cover the top of the cup or mold with a piece of aluminum foil and poke the stick through the foil. Freeze for 3 to 4 hours and enjoy!

# MASON JAR FLOWERPOTS

When I think of picnics, I think of fresh air and flowers. I thought it would be a nice touch to have the kids make their own flowerpots out of mason jars and clay pots. Not only were the kids inspired, they produced their own masterpieces, which their parents loved.

2 tablespoons each of various colors of acrylic paint per kid

1 paintbrush per paint color

1 mason jar or clay flowerpot per kid

1 cup of soil per kid

1 or more flowers per kid

Lay out an array of paints and brushes. Use mason jars and clay pots for the kids to decorate. Have the kids paint their favorite designs and artwork. Let the creative journey begin— they won't need any more direction than that. Let the newly decorated pots dry, then give each kid soil and one or more flowers to plant inside the pot.

# SACK RACE

Create a starting point and finish line for your sack race using tape or another object—we used our tree as the end point. You can find burlap sacks online and at some gardening stores. Have each kid pick a sack and place both feet inside it at the starting line. Call out a countdown or wave a flag to start the race. Now all the kids have to do is hop inside their sacks to the finish line.

=== TIPS ===

- When they're making the ice pops, have the kids write a secret message using something nontoxic on the stick. They can get creative and write their names, initials, or a quote.

- Reading and doing educational activities are nice additions to a picnic. This is a great way for us to work on an assignment in a stress-free environment.

# So Totally Eighties

As many of you know, I am obsessed with the eighties. I absolutely love the era and hold it very close to my heart. People often ask me if I ever get sick of being referred to as Punky, and the answer is NO! Punky will always be a part of who I am, and I still see her in me. I love that she was someone who people loved and cared about and that she also encouraged others to be individuals and to not be afraid to be who they are. So many of the lessons that she taught me and others are lessons that still hold true today. My love for the eighties runs so deep that for my birthday, I was inspired to do an eighties prom. I am obsessed with John Hughes movies and eighties music and decor. The whole thing gets me super-excited, so of course we had to kick off the night celebrating with my little ones, eighties prom style! My husband even broke out his varsity jacket from high school.

# SLOPPY JOES

One of my closest friends is the amazing chef Jon Shook. He is incredible. He and his business partner, Vinny Dotolo, have two of the most delicious restaurants in Los Angeles: Animal and Son of a Gun. If you are visiting the city, I highly recommend going. I have known Jon and Vinny for years, and they are truly special. Jon has been in our home for birthdays for us and our kids, anniversaries, and holidays. I feel so lucky to have great friends, but to also have friends who have the magical touch to create feasts is really unique. I got so excited when I asked Jon to share a few recipes for this book and he said yes. I almost screamed in excitement on the phone. Now I get to share a little of the magic with you.

**YIELD: 6 SERVINGS**

1 pound lean ground beef

¼ cup chopped onion

¼ cup chopped green bell pepper

½ teaspoon garlic powder

1 teaspoon French's yellow mustard

¾ cup ketchup

4 teaspoons brown sugar

Salt, to taste

6 French rolls

Brown the ground beef with the onion and green pepper, then drain off the liquid. Put the beef back in the pot and add the garlic powder, mustard, ketchup, and sugar. Turn the heat down to low and cook for 15 to 20 minutes. Add salt to taste. Divide the mixture evenly among the French rolls.

# PHOTO COLLAGE

One of the hits of the party was our photo collage with my favorite eighties heartthrobs. When I was a kid, my bedroom walls were covered with pictures of all of my childhood crushes. So I took this obsession to the walls of my party and decked them out.

**WHAT YOU'LL NEED**

Images of favorite eighties stars

Photo paper

1 pair scissors

Tape

Old frames or large piece of card stock

Print photos of your favorite eighties images. Fold, cut, or tear the images into the perfect collection of shapes. Tape them into an old frame or on a large piece of card stock. Another fun addition is to pull old prom pictures from the Internet or the family collection to add to the collage.

# LAVA BOTTLES

Whenever I think of the eighties, lava lamps come to mind. I remember my purple lava lamp from when I was growing up. I loved it. This craft is super-fun and is like going back in time. It is also a great opportunity to teach kids a little about science, like how water and oil don't mix. Or to have a chat about your own youth . . .

1 (20-ounce) clear plastic bottle per kid

4 ounces water per kid

5 to 8 drops food coloring per kid

14 ounces baby oil per kid

1 pinch of glitter per kid (optional)

1 fizzy antacid tablet per kid

Clean out a 20-ounce clear plastic bottle and fill with about 4 ounces of water. Add 5 to 8 drops of the food coloring of your choice and mix. The more food coloring you add, the more vibrant the color of the lava bottle. Add roughly 14 ounces of baby oil. This should fill the bottle to the shoulder. If your kid loves glitter, add it now. Break or cut the antacid tablet into halves and drop the two pieces into the bottle. Screw on the top, and watch the show. Flip the bottle over and back to separate the layers.

# DANCE FREEZE GAME

As I mentioned, I *love* eighties music. There's nothing like putting on "Safety Dance" or some Madonna to have a dance party. One of my favorite things to do with the kids is to play some of my favorite hits from the eighties. They have a few favorites too—"Happy Birthday" eighties-style and "Hey Mickey." It's a great way for parents and their kids to bond.

Put on your favorite eighties song. While the music is playing, have the kids perform their favorite eighties moves—the moonwalk, the Cabbage Patch kid, and the robot, to name a few. When the music stops, the kids freeze in their dance positions. Whoever doesn't stop dancing when you turn off your stereo is out. The last kid still on the dance floor at the end of the game wins eighties-inspired goodies. Fun prizes can be eighties toys like Rubik's Cubes and jelly bracelets.

═══════════════ TIPS ═══════════════

- Adding a photo booth to any party is a sure way to create lasting memories. To create your homemade booth, all you need is a sheet or a large piece of fabric to make a backdrop—you can use a rope with clothespins or tape or simply drape the fabric. A friend can play photographer, and there are great apps that create photo-booth strips. It is fun to put up signs with your favorite eighties sayings like "RAD" and "TOTALLY AWESOME." You can have the kids hold the signs up while they are having their pictures taken.

- As a nice touch, create name tags for your guests to wear. We used the name tags to help us vote for a prom king and queen. A friend of ours stood at the door and kept track of each person and what costume he or she was wearing so we could vote later.

- We had all eighties music playing and did one another's hair and makeup beforehand. My girlfriend brought corsages, and the girls went crazy for them. One of the true highlights was getting ready together.

RAINBOW PARTY

OW CAKE POPS rainbow ice JEWEL
ED T-SHIRTS pin the gold on the rain
CAKE BA RAINBOW CA
ow ice TIE-D
e gold CAKE
RAINBOW JEW
IN the go
RA
b w ic
rai e go
RTS r RA
y bar w CU
KING TI nbow ic
ow CUPC pin the go
rainbow ice JEWELRY MAKING
RTS pin the gold on the rainbow CU

CHAPTER
**15**

# Somewhere Over the Rainbow

I was so excited when Poet said that she wanted to throw a rainbow party. I had been spending a lot of time on Pinterest and inspiration boards inspired by the rainbow excitement going on around the Web. So I literally jumped up and down when she enthusiastically announced that this is what she wanted to do for her birthday. There was a whole rainbow waiting to be explored, and the options were endless. It was also a super-fun party to plan with the little ones. I really feel that the more you encourage kids to be a part of the entire process, the more fun the whole party is, especially if there are siblings. It's a way to involve them in the process and make them feel included and special.

# RAINBOW CAKE POPS

My friends from Cake Divas make delicious and beautiful cakes and treats. They shared their special cake-pop recipe with me so that we could all make them at home! For an easy version, you can use a boxed cake mix and canned frosting. Have fun, and experiment with flavors!

**YIELD: 36 CAKE POPS**

**SIMPLE VANILLA CAKE**

1 cup granulated sugar

½ cup butter, melted

2 eggs

2 teaspoons vanilla extract

1½ cups all-purpose flour

1¾ teaspoons baking powder

½ cup milk

½ cup store-bought confetti sprinkles (optional)

The day before you plan to make the cake pops, bake the Simple Vanilla Cake. Preheat oven to 350°F degrees, and grease and flour an 8-by-8-inch pan. Cream together the sugar and melted butter. Mix in eggs, vanilla extract, flour, and baking powder. Stir in milk until the batter is smooth. For a fun "rainbow" twist, add ⅓ cup store-bought confetti sprinkles to the mix, if desired. Place batter in prepared pan.

Bake 30 to 40 minutes, or until toothpick inserted into center comes out clean. Refrigerate overnight.

**TO MAKE THE POPS**
1 batch Simple Vanilla Cake
(recipe on previous page)

4 ounces cream cheese,
softened

2 tablespoons butter, melted

1 cup powdered sugar

1 tablespoon milk

36 lollipop sticks (available at
craft store or grocery baking
aisle)

24 ounces white-chocolate
almond bark and food coloring
to make assorted colors for

dipping, OR 24 ounces of
dipping chocolate in various
colors (available at craft store
or grocery baking aisle)

Flavor sprinkles, if desired
(optional)

Break up the refrigerated cake into a large
bowl. Crumble it with a fork into fine crumbs.
In a separate bowl, whip together the cream
cheese, butter, powdered sugar, and milk
until smooth. Pour the mixture into the cake
crumbs and mix with a spoon until well
blended. Refrigerate until firm and a molding
consistency.

Cover a baking sheet with wax paper. Take
a tablespoonful of the cake mixture and roll
it into a smooth ball. Insert a lollipop stick,
pointing upward, as you put the ball back
down on the sheet. When all 36 sticks have
been used, put the baking sheet in the freezer
for about 20 minutes so that the balls harden.

Melt chocolate in a double boiler on the
stove or in the microwave. Add colors to the
chocolate, as needed, in different coffee cups.
Carefully dip the pops, adding optional flavor
sprinkles before the chocolate hardens. It is
helpful to have a small piece of Styrofoam
handy to insert the pop sticks into to dry,
right side up. If you don't have this, you can
let the pops dry on the baking sheet, with the
stick up.

# RAINBOW ICE

This recipe is perfect anytime because you can use bottled juices you already have in your fridge, or you can use fresh fruit and make your own juices! We love using organic ingredients, but to show the kids how bright and colorful we could turn the ice cubes, we added a few drops of food coloring.

## YIELD: 10 ICE CUBES

2 tablespoons pineapple juice

2 tablespoons orange juice

2 tablespoons white grape juice

2 tablespoons grape juice

2 tablespoons fruit punch

2 tablespoons blueberry juice

Food coloring (optional)

Ice-cube tray

Mix each fruit juice with a drop or two of the appropriate-colored food coloring, if desired. Once you have the juices ready, place them into the ice-cube tray in a perfect rainbow order—red, orange, yellow, green, blue, and purple—and freeze for 3 to 4 hours.

# TIE-DYED T-SHIRTS

Tie-dye can be so awesome—and so very messy. The girls really wanted to do a tie-dye station, and everyone got really into it. We did get dye all over, but we'd thought ahead and put down a tarp below the station. Mess and all, it was definitely a blast!

1 cup soda ash

16 cups warm water

2 tablespoons each of various fabric dye colors

7 (8-ounce) squirt bottles

1 to 5 rubber bands per kid

1 T-shirt per kid

2 clothespins per kid

1 rope and clothespins to hang shirts to dry

There are a few variations of tie-dyeing. We used the squirt bottle method because it's the easiest for kids. You can provide old aprons or clothes to make this process as clean as possible. There are a few things you can do to prepare the night before. First, dissolve the soda ash in warm water in a jug according to the directions. Soda ash can be found at most craft stores. Next, mix 2 tablespoons of each dye color with 3 ounces water inside separate squirt bottles. Do not mix the soda ash water and dye together until you are ready to start the tie-dyeing process.

Once the kids are about to tie-dye, top off each squirt bottle of dye with 4 ounces of soda ash water. Now all the kids have to do is rubber band their shirts in sections and squirt on whatever color dye they like. After they are done, undo the rubber bands, use clothespins to clip the shirts to the rope, and let the art pieces soak up the sun.

# JEWELRY MAKING

My girls love making jewelry. It is an activity that is fun for the whole family. We can sit for hours beading. So break out the rainbow colors and start working on those beautiful jewelry creations. This is a perfect take-home gift, something that my kids love!

7 mason jars for beads

20 to 50 beads per bracelet or necklace

1 (12-inch) colored string for bracelet per kid

1 (22-inch) colored string for necklace per kid

1 pair of craft scissors

Separate beads in designated mason jars in a rainbow fashion: red, orange, yellow, green, blue, purple, and pink. Precut the strings to bracelet (10–12 inches) and necklace (20–22 inches) sizes. Knot one end of the string about 1 inch up and allow the kids to string beads in their own colorful way. When they are done, knot the other end of the string, then tie both ends together to form a necklace or a bracelet. Trim any excess string.

# CUPCAKE BAR

You and the little ones can make cupcakes with icing before the party. Then set up fun rainbow colors and goodies for the kids to decorate with and make their own creations.

# CANDY BAR

Mason jars are one of my favorite must-haves when throwing a party. Take candy and divide it by color into different mason jars, then add a spoon or scooper for the candy. We also use rubber-stamped hangtags to add some flair and style.

## TIPS

- Place colored balloons—the bigger the better—around the house and backyard. I love using super-bright colored balloons and bringing them together to create a rainbow.

- I am obsessed with striped straws. They make any party more classic looking.

- I love supporting local small businesses, momtrepeneurs, and crafters online. You can find amazing things for your party on the Internet. See my reference guide at the end of the book.

- We have some super-great craft ideas on moonfrye.com.

# PIN THE GOLD ON THE RAINBOW

This game was inspired by the classic Pin the Tail on the Donkey. I love to take games from my childhood and make them into something new my girls can relate to. It was so much fun for the kids to play this game. The kids got such a thrill seeing how close they were to getting their gold coin in the pot.

Craft paper

Paint

Cotton balls

Glue

Gold coins

Double-sided tape

Bandanna

Paint a rainbow, about 3 feet in size, on a piece of craft paper. Use cotton balls and glue to add clouds at the bottom. Paint a bucket at the start or end of the rainbow with black paint— don't worry, you don't need to be an artist for this one! The empty black bucket makes the perfect target to pin the gold coins to. Hang your rainbow so the kids can reach it easily. Hand a gold coin, prepped with double-sided tape, to each kid. You can find gold coins at local novelty, craft or toy stores. Use a bandanna as a blindfold, spin the kid around a few times, and point him or her toward the rainbow. The kid who gets the gold coin "in" or closest to the black pot is the winner. There can be more than one winner, if the black pot fills.

# CHAPTER 16

# Take Me Out to the Ball Game

I don't have boys, but I grew up with brothers. I learned how to throw a football at an early age. My husband jokes that while I may not be very athletic, I still know how to throw a ball. Many of my friends spend weekends running around from baseball games to soccer fields with their sons and daughters, so there's no better way to celebrate a birthday for your little athlete than with a fun sports party.

# RICE KRISPIES BASEBALLS

Treats made with Rice Krispies remind me so much of being a kid. Not only are they fast and easy to make, but they are delicious. I knew I wanted to incorporate a creative twist on them in the book. When we planned this sports party, I immediately thought: baseball Rice Krispies! The kids loved decorating them, and so did I.

### YIELD: 12–15 BALLS

- 4 tablespoons butter
- 6 cups marshmallows
- 6 cups Kellogg's Rice Krispies cereal
- 2 cups white-chocolate morsels
- 2 tablespoons shortening
- Red icing
- Parchment paper

Melt butter in a large saucepan over low heat. Add marshmallows and stir until they are completely melted and a smooth consistency. Remove from heat and stir in the Rice Krispies until well coated. Once the mixture is cooled, wet your hands and roll it into balls. Place the balls on parchment paper. While the baseballs harden, melt the white-chocolate morsels and shortening in a saucepan, on low heat. Stir frequently, and remove from heat when it has melted together. Use a fork to dip the cereal balls into the melted morsels. Coat well with white chocolate and place on parchment paper to set. Once chocolate is hardened, draw on the baseball stitching with red icing.

# CUSTOM JERSEYS

Every athlete needs a jersey, so have each kid transform a T-shirt into his or her very own customized jersey, using an array of fabric paints! Let each kid design their own team name and mascot, or collaborate together and come up with a wild team name everyone will love! A team cheer and a game or two will definitely be in order. The kids will love seeing their new jerseys in action!

1 white T-shirt per kid

2 tablespoons each of various colors fabric paint

1 paintbrush for each color

Set out white shirts in different sizes for each kid to choose, making sure to include a good amount of each size. I got mine from Target, where they have a great, affordable selection. Once the kids pick out their shirts, have them paint away. Let them pick their own numbers for the back of the shirt so when the games begin they will each have a designated number. Hang the shirts to dry, using clothespins, for 1 to 2 hours.

# SPORTS GAME

A fun game of baseball or football is an awesome activity for a sports-themed birthday. Getting together at a park for a game is a great way to throw a fun, affordable party where people are interacting and friends and family can spend quality time being active and outside together. Parents can play too—just make sure not to get so competitive that it takes the fun out of it for the little ones. It's not about who wins or loses, just how much fun you have playing the game.

## TIPS

- To save money, you can buy chips in bulk and place them in brown paper bags for individual servings. A rubber-stamped brown paper bag of chips adds a dash of style. To create a classic look, fold the top of your paper bag down two inches before filling with chips. Line the bag with a paper towel to absorb the oil from the chips.

- A good reminder for any sports party is to make sure you have plenty of liquids and sunscreen on hand.

# STAMPED BASEBALLS

1 baseball per kid

Baseball-inspired or team rubber stamp

Assorted colored ink pads

As you can see in photographs throughout the book, I love a great rubber stamp. My girlfriend Lisa rubber-stamped her son's team name on their baseballs. I love this idea. It looks amazing and builds team spirit too, which is so important to foster in young ones! You can get custom rubber stamps made for your kids' teams. Rubber stamps and ink pads are available at most craft stores. I especially love the special ones I find at Paper Source.

# Cha Cha Cha

Mexico is one of our favorite places to go as a family. The kids love doing crafts by the ocean, getting their hair braided, and hanging out on the beach. Punta Mita is a beautiful place, and we love visiting the small town of Sayulita. Jagger talks about Mexico on a regular basis, and she was set on having a fiesta to celebrate her fourth birthday. Jagger's fiesta included everything she loved about our trips to Mexico—from the food to the music and the activities. My friend Jon brought over an authentic Mexican feast. We broke out the maracas, got some piñatas downtown, and our fiesta was born.

# GUACAMOLE

My girls love fresh guacamole. We have spent a lot of weekends making this guacamole in our house. It always makes a delicious snack that the kids enjoy time and time again.

### YIELD: 6–8 SERVINGS

3 large fresh avocados, peeled and pitted

1 Roma tomato, chopped

¼ teaspoon salt

Splash of lemon juice

Slice the avocados into a bowl. Mix with a fork until pieces are the right consistency. I like my guacamole chunky. Stir in the chopped tomato and salt. Sprinkle lemon juice on top and serve fresh.

# MARACAS

Every fiesta needs maracas! Without them, the party is a little less exciting than it could be. Blank wooden maracas make the perfect canvas for your child's artwork and create the musical spirit every fiesta should include.

1 set of blank wooden maracas per kid

2 tablespoons each of various colors paint

1 paintbrush per color

2 to 4 pinches of glitter (optional)

Set out paint, brushes, and glitter, along with blank wooden maracas. Have the kids paint their favorite designs, colors, and artwork. Glitter is a great way to spice up the maracas. If the kids choose this sparkled addition, have them sprinkle the glitter over the wet paint so it will stay on with every shake. In the end, the kids will have the perfect musical instruments for their fiesta.

# PIÑATAS

My girlfriend and I went downtown to find the perfect piñata for the party. Jagger loves piñatas so much that we gave her a special cupcake piñata for a birthday present. It's such a fun activity to do. Just be careful. When it rained during Jagger's birthday, it turned into a muddy extravaganza.

=== TIPS ===

- Fill your gift bags with unique, colorful, and authentic goodies.

- If you want an alternative to candy and are having a party in the evening, glow bracelets are a great option. My brother had a piñata at his kid's birthday, and they had it filled with glow bracelets. It was a smashing hit.

# Little Explorers

One thing I've learned since having children is that my little ones love to explore. Anytime they have the chance, they want to run outside and play adventure games. The idea behind a "little explorers" party is to create a fun environment where your kids can explore away! From obstacle courses to hide-and-seek, you can create areas indoors or outdoors that are fun and safe for them to play in. Whether they want to get dressed up in fancy dresses like my girls or get decked out in camouflage like my friends' sons, the little explorers can be a fun party for everyone.

# ANTS ON A LOG

This simple combination of kid-friendly ingredients will give the little adventurers the energy to complete their journey. I love this recipe because it combines the healthy with small toppings of sweets. In our house we use almond butter, but peanut butter can be substituted. Don't be surprised if you run out of the ants on a log—sometimes the simplest things in life are the best.

### YIELD: 8–12 LOGS

4 stalks celery, trimmed

½ cup almond butter

¼ cup raisins and/or chocolate chips

Clean the celery thoroughly with cool water. Cut the stalks into halves or thirds depending on the length. Spread almond butter on the inside, and sprinkle with raisins and/or chocolate chips. Yummy *and* fun to eat!

# FACE PAINTING

1 stick of green face paint
1 stick of brown face paint
1 stick of black face paint
Paintbrush (optional)

Face painting can be intricate, but not when it comes to the rogue type of face painting. Grab brown, black, and green face paints, and have a field day. Use your fingers or a paintbrush to create designs on the kids faces. You don't need to be a professional to do this. The more abstract the design, the better it will mask your kiddos on their hide-and-seek adventure! Some kids may like it simple, with only black lines under their eyes, and others will love the combination of greens mixed with darker colors—think camouflage patterns.

# HIDE-AND-SEEK

We love a good old-fashioned game of hide-and-seek. Nothing like the giggling of kids hiding from one another while running around the house. For our little explorers party, my friends' kids came over, and the boys, with painted faces, put on camouflage costumes and hid throughout the backyard. They broke out the flashlights and went on an adventure.

TIPS

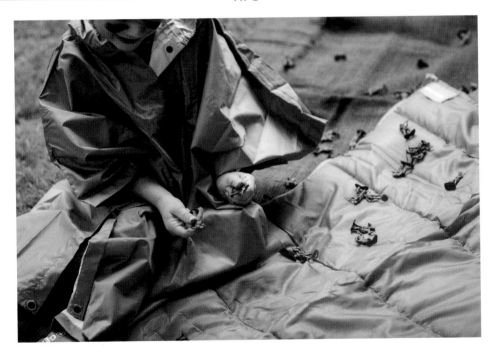

- Sleeping bags are a really fun addition to the little explorers party. The boys sat on them and played for hours.

- Gather flashlights, compasses, and other items to help set off your adventure.

- Create an obstacle course around the backyard for the kids to complete.

- Have kids arrive in their favorite camouflage costumes.

# Ghoulish Times

I love Halloween—it's one of my very favorite holidays. We didn't have much money growing up, but my mom always made it special, even on a tight budget. She would put dry ice on the front lawn to make it look spooky, and she decorated our house in a way that made all of the kids want to come over. My favorite costume was when she made me into the Statue of Liberty using tinfoil! It was simple, homemade, and perfect. For this party, we used fun, innovative ways to decorate pumpkins, a Halloween-inspired game, and the perfect way to make caramel apples a creative process. Other ideas for a Halloween party include changing classic games and snacks into spooky-inspired ones.

# CARAMEL APPLE BAR

I had such a blast with the girls when we made caramel apples. They were part of the whole creative process, from picking the toppings and helping organize them to decorating their own apples in the most amazing ways. The girls even started to art-direct me on what toppings I should add and where to add them!

### YIELD: 6 CARAMEL APPLES

6 apples (green or red)

6 sticks for apples

Parchment paper

1 package of individually wrapped caramels

2 tablespoons water

**TOPPINGS**

1 cup mini marshmallows

1 cup mini chocolate chips

1 cup mini M&Ms

1 cup chopped walnuts

1 cup shredded coconut

1 cup sprinkles

Remove the stems and insert the sticks at the top, three-quarters of the way into each apple. Lightly grease parchment paper and place on a baking sheet or tray. Unwrap the caramels and place into a saucepan with the water on low heat, stirring frequently. Once melted and smooth, remove from heat. Dip each apple into the caramel sauce and coat well. Let the excess caramel drip off, then decorate with your favorite toppings. Place each apple on the parchment paper. Now all you have to do is wait for the caramel to cool and harden to enjoy.

# PUMPKIN DECORATION

This past Halloween, we really got into trying new things with our pumpkins, so we tested three different types of craft paints and decorations. When I was a kid, my dad would paint the most beautiful images on our pumpkins and cut out unbelievable faces. Halloween was a big deal in our house, and I love passing on those same traditions to my girls now. I hold the memories of Halloween really close to my heart, and I hope they will too.

**Painting pumpkins.** My kids love painting pumpkins. It's safe, fun, and easy to do. Even the littlest Halloween lovers can participate without being shooed away from sharp knives, candles, and carving tools. Bring out the acrylic paint and let your kids be young Picassos.

**Chalkboard pumpkins!** Spray-paint your pumpkin black, making sure no orange shows through. Then paint it again with chalkboard paint. Once the chalkboard paint is dry, you can draw pictures and write messages in chalk. Try using multiple pumpkins to create sentences or words. This is a perfect way to make your house stand out on Halloween night!

**Pumpkins in tights.** Another fun decoration for your pumpkins is wrapping them in old stockings. I somehow always manage to get a run in my tights. Instead of throwing ruined stockings away, you can stash them somewhere—you never know when they might come in handy for crafting! Take your stocking and cut it to the desired height depending on the size of your pumpkin. Tie fabric at top. If you want to get more creative, you can add festive Halloween pins to the stocking.

# CANDY BAG STAMPING

Find fun stamps that will show off the kids' unique personalities. Do you have a princess lover or a skeleton junkie? There's a stamp out there that will be perfect for everyone. Let them put their mark—literally—on the goodie bags their friends will take home. This craft is a fun and easy way to get the kids involved in their own party planning and to allow them to feel proud of their creations when it's time to say good-bye.

1 blank paper bag per kid
Selection of rubber stamps
Orange and black ink pads

Put out several blank paper bags for kids to decorate. Lay out a display of different rubber stamps, from Halloween-inspired to numbers and letters, and orange and black ink pads. Give them a nice array of different colored inks. Have them stamp their hearts away and create the perfect candy bag to fill up during the party.

# PUMPKIN POLO

Using a broom, a craft pumpkin, and masking tape, create your own pumpkin polo match. What is pumpkin polo? Well, it's actually simpler than it sounds. Use a broom to sweep the pumpkin into the goal for a score. Think hockey, but in an innocent Halloween way. Make a goal using tape, and let the games begin. Depending on how many kids you have, the number of players on the field changes. If there are only two kids, it becomes one-on-one. If there are six kids, then each team can have a goalie and two players trying to score a goal.

=== TIPS ===

- I love decorating and almost all of our decorations came from Target.

- Definitely have the kids help put up the Halloween decorations—my girls always surprise me with just how creative and innovative they are.

- It's a fun time to tell scary stories (not *too* scary!) and bond with your kids.

- Set up a station where, without looking, the kids can put their hands into "eyeballs" (peeled grapes) and "guts" (slime). It never seems to get old in our house!

# A Thanksgiving to Be Grateful For

We talk to our little ones about being grateful throughout the year, but Thanksgiving is a great time to really focus as a family on all we are thankful for. I love to cook and usually start the day off super-early in the kitchen. I involve the kids and try to make it fun for the whole family. One really important thing that my mom taught me on Thanksgiving was to give back. When I was as young as seven, my mom would take me to downtown Los Angeles the day before Thanksgiving to feed the homeless. This tradition taught me the importance of giving back and sharing that with my girls.

# GREEN BEANS

I love making green beans. They're one of our favorites! Every holiday we do green beans, and they make an awesome side dish to complement all the other delicious food on the menu. They're always one of the first things to disappear!

**YIELD: 6 SERVINGS**

1 pounds fresh green beans, trimmed

2 tablespoons butter

1 teaspoon salt

Boil the green beans for half an hour, until they're super soft, and slather them in the butter. Toss them with the salt—feel free to add more. I love salty foods.

# PINECONE HOLDERS

1 pinecone per kid

Selection of crayons

1 piece of card stock per kid

Selection of stamps

This is a simple, fun craft, and it's super festive. Place the pinecone on its side and stick three crayons between the scales on each side. This is a festive way to color during your Thanksgiving dinner. Kids love having their names in front of them, so make a place card with their name stamped onto it.

Recently we were in India on an incredible adventure, meeting the Dalai Lama. The kids had an amazing time, and it was a great bonding experience. We went to visit small villages, rode on camels, met children of all ages, and saw the world in a whole new way. We spent Thanksgiving in Rhajasthan at the truly beautiful hotel where we were staying, the Amanbaugh. They were so kind and made us a Thanksgiving feast. I loved the way they wrote the menu on banana leaves, which is an idea I would love to include in a party soon. Special thanks to everyone at the Aman for making it so special. My children had the trip of a lifetime, and we all came home inspired by the magical journey.

# THANKFUL STONE

1 stone per kid
1 or 2 gold metallic pens

Have each child use a metallic pen to write one thing he or she is thankful for on the stone. Share your stone messages with each other during dinner, and have the kids keep the stone to remind them of what they are thankful for during the rest of the year. We collected stones from our own backyard.

# THANKFUL TURKEY COLORING

On thick card stock, design Thanksgiving themes. You can have kids cut these out of magazines, print them from the computer, or color and cut out their own turkey designs. Leave a space on the card below the turkey image for each child to write in a caption and decorate.

TIPS

- During Thanksgiving, the girls and I try to participate in the local food drives. It's a great way to help others. Get involved in your own community in any way that you can.

- It doesn't matter where you are, you can always celebrate what you're thankful for.

- I love to make personalized place cards for the holidays. For the place card shown above, I used a thin wooden cutout and glitter glue to write the kids' names.

# CHAPTER 21

# A Holiday to Remember

When you grow up with a chef for a mom, holidays are the best time of year. My whole family and extended family came together on holidays to celebrate and eat my mom's delicious creations. Food was one of the amazing ways my mother used to express herself, and that creative spirit made the holidays extra-special. Our house was the party house, the one where everyone gathered and celebrated. People would come and roast chestnuts on the front lawn and gather around singing. It was so much fun. As I grew up, the traditions continued. My best friend and I have come together to throw a Christmas Eve celebration every year for as long as I can remember. I love the holidays so much!

# MASHED POTATOES

One of our favorite traditions from this time of year is the mashed potatoes. Over the years, our mashed potatoes have become legendary, and people look forward to them all year long. We each take turns adding a dash of garlic salt here, a spoonful of sour cream there, so the recipe is never exact, but it's always super-yummy. During the rest of the year whenever my family needs a little extra TLC, I'll make a batch of those mashed potatoes.

## YIELD: 6 SERVINGS

4 large russet potatoes, peeled and cut in halves

¼ cup milk

⅓ cup sour cream

1 stick of salted butter (I personally like to add a little more to taste)

½ teaspoon salt

Garlic salt (optional)

Boil water in a medium-large pot and add peeled potatoes. Drain the water once the potatoes are soft. Add the milk, sour cream, butter, and salt, plus garlic salt, if desired. Mash with a potato masher, adding more salt as necessary. For a thinner consistency, add more milk. Like your mashed potatoes super-creamy? Up the sour cream. The best part about this recipe for mashed potatoes is that you can customize it for your family's taste.

# BUTTERMILK FRIED CHICKEN

One of my absolute holiday favorites is Jon Shook's incredible fried chicken. We ask him for it every season. I am so excited that he is sharing the recipe with us for the book! I know all of my friends are going to be rushing to make it. I can't wait to hear how all of you like it.

## YIELD: 6 SERVINGS

6 chicken breast pieces (4–5 ounces each)

2 cups buttermilk

1 cup all-purpose flour (plus more if needed)

1 tablespoon fine black pepper

3 cups canola oil

1 tablespoon salt

Two to three days before cooking, place chicken breast pieces in a large resealable plastic bag with the buttermilk, seal tightly, and refrigerate two to three days. Place the flour and black pepper in a large bowl and mix. Pull one chicken piece from the buttermilk and put it into the flour mixture. Dredge both sides really well. Place the coated chicken on a plate. Repeat for all pieces.

Heat the canola oil in a pot over medium heat to 345°F. Add coated chicken to the pot, and cook for 8 minutes. Transfer the chicken to a paper towel, and season with salt. Let the chicken stand for 15 to 20 minutes after it is fried before eating.

# SNOW GLOBES

- 1 mason jar or clear plastic lidded container per kid
- 1 toy tree per kid
- 1 bottle Gorilla Glue or glue gun
- 1 to 2 cups distilled water per kid
- 1 tablespoon of glycerin per kid
- 1 to 2 tablespoons of glitter per kid

Let it snow with this wonderfully festive craft! Whether it's constantly shaken, a keepsake, or decor for the holiday table, this craft is too nostalgic to pass up. There are two versions of this craft: the mason jar or the eco-friendly recycled plastic container. Either way, it will provide a smile for adults and kids. So grab your container of choice, and let's get started . . .

Wash and dry your jar. Attach your tree using Gorilla Glue or a glue gun. Let it dry for an hour or two. Add distilled water and the glycerin until the container is almost full; the solution should be 1 inch from the top. The next part was my girls' favorite—adding the glitter! We gave them a selection to add to their majestic snow globes—the bigger the glitter the better. Of course they added as much glitter as they could get away with—'tis the spirit!

If you're using a mason jar, you won't need to seal the lid with glue. However, if recycling a plastic container, make sure to seal the lid using glue to avoid leakage. Now just shake away! (But be careful with the glass, as we have had snow-globe accidents in our house.)

# DREIDELS

1 (1½- to 2-inch) wood block per kid

1 (1-inch) candle cup knob per kid

1 (1-inch) wood ball head knob per kid

2 tablespoons each of various paint colors

1 paintbrush per color

1 bottle Gorilla Glue or glue gun

Dreidel, dreidel, dreidel, I made it out of wood . . . Create this homemade dreidel out of a few easy-to-find wood products. All you have to do is use Gorilla Glue or a glue gun to attach the candle cup tops and ball head knobs. This is best to do the day before, but if you want the kids to help on the day of the party, then let the glue dry for an hour before you move on to the painting fun. Have the kids paint the sides of their dreidels with their favorite colors, then set aside to dry. This is a perfect opportunity to teach them the Hebrew alphabet that will be represented on their dreidel (nun, gimel, hey, and shin), together representing the spirit of Hanukkah. Let them paint one letter on each side of their dreidel. Once dry, let the games begin!

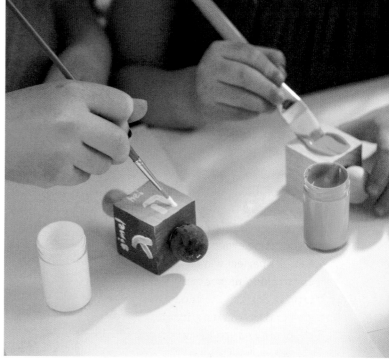

# PAPER ORNAMENT

1 piece card stock per kid

2 to 3 pinches of glitter per ornament

1 bottle nontoxic glue

For the holiday you can create a cute paper ornament by cutting out card stock and decorating it however you'd like. Glue is a perfect way to write on your kids' names or draw favorite designs. Just add some glue, sprinkle on the glitter, shake off, and you'll have the perfect craft ornament.

# TWELVE NIGHTS OF CHRISTMAS AND SECRET SANTA GAME

My Christmas would never be complete without two key elements: the "Twelve Nights of Christmas" sing-along and a game of Secret Santa. On Christmas Eve as our guests are arriving, we pass out two slips of paper to each family member: One is a printed line of lyrics from the song, and the other is a number. After dinner, we gather everyone together and sing the song, with each family member singing the line on his or her slip of paper. It's no time to be shy—the louder and sillier you sing the lyrics, the better. My big brother always gets "five golden rings" and really belts it out; each year he does it louder and with more feeling. It's a moment I look forward to all year long. The kids love it, and the parents might love it even more!

After we've all sung our hearts out, it's time for Secret Santa. The kids take turns reading off numbers, and one grown-up from each family comes forward to claim the gift with the corresponding number. The next person whose number is called can either "steal" the present that came before his or hers or choose a new one. If they pick a new one, they must open it immediately—and then the next person can steal that present or open a new one. The numbers continue, with each subsequent person opting to either steal from someone before them or to pick a new present. It's chaotic, with people calling one another out and teasing one another, but all in good fun. In the end, everyone ends up with something great, and we all have a blast playing!

## TIPS

- The girls love to decorate platters with flowers. It is a fun way to involve the kids. Have your little helpers pick out different ways to make any dish look festive. Just make sure the flowers are kid-safe.

- I have great memories of my dad bringing us presents on Christmas morning wrapped in tinfoil. He would make his world-famous fudge and wrap it with tinfoil and a bow. It really made our day! One way to reuse and make super-cool wrapping paper is to tear out the old pages of a newspaper or magazine, wrap your gift, and tie it with a bow.

- Every Christmas Eve, bright and early, my girlfriend and I go to the flower market to pick out our flowers for the holiday. It is something I look forward to year-round. I love getting beautiful, fresh flowers at a great price. Look into local flower markets or farmers' markets to get great deals.

# Acknowledgments

Thank you to everyone who made this book such an amazing experience!

To my husband and kids, I love you beyond words, and you make this life such an incredible adventure! Every day is a party with you. You are my heart, my inspiration, and the most beautiful part of life.

To my mom, who made our home like a summer camp and was the best chef and party planner ever! You always made every experience colorful and full of life, and I thank you for giving me the roots to follow my dreams.

Meeno, my big brother, you are such a visionary, and you have made this book so beautiful with your pictures and touch. I am so grateful to have your brilliant eye to capture the moments of this wonderfully chaotic life.

To my nieces, you are an inspiration always and make life so much more colorful.

Ilse, I love you so much, and I am so grateful for all of your support throughout this process. Your style and design is incredible, and I am so thankful for all of your help. P.S. You have a way with confetti like I have never seen before. This cover is beautiful. Thank you for your continuous magic!

To Andy McNicol, thank you for helping to make this book a reality. I love that you can take my vision and PowerPoint book presentations and share them with the same passion that I have. You are an amazing agent but beyond that, you are a great friend.

To Jennifer Levesque, thank you for spending so much time on this project and pouring your heart and love into this. You have been a terrific editor and your patience and warmth has constantly kept me grounded throughout this experience.

To everyone at Abrams Books, I thank you for believing in this project and for giving it so much love and attention.

To Claire Bamundo, you planned out the release of this book like a rock star and a friend throughout. Thank you for bringing our incredible ideas to life and for making me always feel taken care of.

David Blatty, thank you for being so kind and patient with me. You have been an incredible support and I am thrilled to have been on this journey with you.

Erin Vandeveer, Stefanie Linder, and Amy Sly, thank you for believing in this project and for all of the love and care that you have put into it.

To all of my friends at Target, I thank you from the bottom of my heart for the endless support and kindness that you have shown me. I love being Target's Mommy Ambassador, and I am so proud to work with you. I am also so happy that I got to spend so much time running around Target to pick up goodies that we used throughout this book :)

Ashley Karatsonyi, thank you for the amazing design inspiration throughout this entire process. Your passion and attention to detail is impeccable.  You are truly one of a kind and I am forever grateful to your creative genius. You were a rock for my brother and I and a style guru throughout the process. I love you sincerely and will always remember how much you brought this book to life for me and my family. You can do anything, truly!

Lisa Rowe, I love you and your vision. You are not only an incredible friend who has listened to me every day throughout this journey, but also an endless support of creativity and passion. I love you and how your creativity comes to life. Thank you for sharing your brilliance and heart with me always, I am eternally grateful and I adore you and your family. You make every party special and I am so lucky to have you in my life.

Jenny Feldon, thanks for always being my friend that can take all of my words and give me guidance in the nicest way. You are a constant inspiration throughout and I love you and the loyalty that you forever show me.

Brooke Slavik and Justin Ongert, I love you both madly! To my friends at WME, thank you for the ongoing support!!!!

To my amazing friends who let their kids be part of the party fun, thank you sincerely from the bottom of my heart.

Hillary and Adam, thank you for letting your beautiful girls be a special part of this. Your family is a constant inspiration.

Lauren Chighisola, thank you for being a friend always and testing everything out as my taste tester. You are amazing and I am forever thankful.

Hillary Kaye, what can I say, except I love you.

Jon Shook, thank you for the amazing recipes and for always making our parties delicious and special.

To my incredible godmother, thank you for taking us on the life-changing journey to India, which I was able to share in the book. I love you beyond words!

Tori and Robert, thank you for making the holidays so memorable and for the friendship and love, always.

Cake Divas, thanks for the endless fun cakes.

Jane and Marcus, thank you for letting Lilia step back into the eighties.

To Alecia and Randy, thank you for lending us your kids. They were awesome.

Rebecca and Eric, Billy was magic in here. We love you.

Hopper, thanks for being such a trooper, always.

Ali and James, thanks so much for letting the kids play with us.

Chrissy, it was like summer camp all over again.

Stephanie and David, thank you for sharing your beauties with us.

Kara, I am so excited to have you as my partner and friend and so grateful for your support throughout this journey.

To the team that I get to work with daily building Moonfrye, thank you so much for everything. I love you guys!

To my friends and family, thank you for coming to our parties and filling them with joy and laughter. These are the moments we forever cherish . . . "Now Let's Get This Party Started!"

# Resource Guide

**ANIMAL RESTAURANT**
435 North Fairfax Avenue
Los Angeles, CA 90036
323-782-9225
animalrestaurant.com

**BALLOONSFAST**
Wide selection of sizes and colored balloons.
balloonsfast.com

**CAKE DIVAS**
310-248-2253
cakedivas.com

**CANDLE SOYLUTIONS**
Soy candles, mason jars, and accessories.
candlesoylutions.com

**EL CHAMACO**
Mexican fiesta clothing and decorations.
elchamaco.com

**ERIC BUTERBAUGH FLOWERS**
300 South Doheny Drive
Los Angeles, CA 90048
310-247-7120
ericbuterbaugh.com

**ETSY**
Handmade marketplace.
etsy.com

**GERONIMO**
"Certified Balloonatic and Master Balloon-Trooper."
geronimoballoons.com

**LOS ANGELES FLOWER MART**
766 Wall Street
Los Angeles, CA 90014
213-627-3696

**MARK'S GARDEN**
13838 Ventura Boulevard
Sherman Oaks, CA 91423
818-906-1718
marksgarden.com

**MICHAELS**
Locations throughout the United States.
800-642-4235
michaels.com

**MICHAEL LEVINE FABRIC**
920 Maple Avenue
Los Angeles, California 90015
213-622-6259
mlfabric.com

**MOONFRYE**
Come on over to moonfrye.com to share your creations and get inspired.
www.moonfrye.com

**MOSKATEL'S**
733 San Julian Street
Los Angeles, California 90014
213-689-4830

**ORIENTAL TRADING**
Party supplies, crafts, and decorations.
orientaltrading.com

**PAPER SOURCE**
Locations throughout the United States.
paper-source.com

**S&S WORLDWIDE**
Art and craft supplies.
ssww.com

**TARGET**
Locations throughout the United States.
target.com

# Index